LOCKDOWN MADE ME DO IT

LOCKDOWN MADE ME DO IT

60 QUARANTINE COCKTAILS TO MAKE AT HOME

JASSY DAVIS, LANCE J. MAYHEW,
CECILIA RIOS MURRIETA, COLLEEN GRAHAM
AND AMY ZAVATTO
ILLUSTRATED BY RUBY TAYLOR

HarperCollins*Publishers*

HarperCollins*Publishers*
1 London Bridge Street
London SE1 9GF

HarperCollins*Publishers*
1st Floor, Watermarque Building, Ringsend Road
Dublin 4, Ireland

www.harpercollins.co.uk

First published by HarperCollins*Publishers* as the Made Me Do It series, 2017–2020

10 9 8 7 6 5 4 3 2 1

Prosecco Made Me Do It written by Amy Zavatto
Gin Made Me Do It written by Jassy Davis
Tequila Made Me Do It written by Cecilia Rios Murrieta
Whisky Made Me Do It written by Lance J. Mayhew
Rosé Made Me Do It written by Colleen Graham
Illustrated by Ruby Taylor
Design by Gareth Butterworth, E-Digital Design and Jacqui Caulton

A catalogue record for this book is available from the British Library.

ISBN 978-0-00-852234-6

Printed and bound in China

MIX
Paper from
responsible sources
FSC™ C007454

This book is produced from independently certified FSC™ paper
to ensure responsible forest management.

For more information visit: www.harpercollins.co.uk/green

DISCLAIMER:
This book features recipes that include the optional use of raw eggs.
Consuming raw eggs may increase the risk of food-borne illness.
Individuals who are immunocompromised, pregnant, or elderly should use
caution. Ensure eggs are fresh and meet local food-standard requirements.

Please drink responsibly.

CONTENTS

WHISKY

ROSÉ

INTRODUCTION

Life is better with a cocktail in your hand – and not just because it's full of booze. Sharing a bottle of wine or a few beers with friends is fun. But no matter how mellow everyone gets; the night will always taste a little *ordinary*. Take the same people, prop them up in a bar with a round of ice-cold Martinis and the night will always feel more fun, more glamorous and more exciting. This is because cocktails give life its glitter.

These days, while we wait at home for lockdown to lift, a trip to your local hot spot is out of the question. When quarantine is over, we can visit our favourite bars and pubs again. But until then, we have to glitz up our own lives. This is where the cocktail comes in. A Quarantini, if you will.

Your kitchen is only ever one rum cocktail away from being a tiki bar. Your living room just needs a pair of Spritzes to turn it into an Italian trattoria. Your hallway can be an old-fashioned members' club in London, full of whisky and gossip, while your bathroom makes a great stand-in for Miami – as long as you take a Mojito into the tub.

With the right drink, you can conjure up every chic city bar or rustic seaside shack you've ever dreamt of drinking in. I don't recommend trying to visit them all in one night – cocktails are best taken in small doses – but with the recipes in this book, you can enjoy a perfect night out while staying safely in.

We've put these cocktails together because not only can they take you round the world in a glass, they don't require too many trips to the shops. These are paired-down drinks made with a few select,

7

easy-to-source ingredients and the kind of liquors inhabiting everyone's drinks cabinet – as well as a few iconic cocktails to try, should you happen to have some seldom-used bitters or a long-lost vermouth collecting dust. You can get a bit technical with some of the cocktails, and add a few bartender twists, or keep it loose and simple. Make Gin Rickeys with vodka, Whisky Flips with brandy, and Margaritas with white rum. Now is the time for experiments and having fun. And who knows? Maybe lockdown will help you invent a new cocktail classic.

SYRUPS, PURÉES AND INFUSIONS

Many cocktails in this book require a touch of simple syrup. I prefer using this to caster sugar or any granulated sugar, no matter how fine, because it's already dissolved and easier to mix with. Make a batch ahead of time and store it in your refrigerator. The variations you can make on this are only limited by your imagination and ingredients, but here are the recipes contained in this book for your reference.

SIMPLE SYRUP

The basic recipe tells you a lot about the name: it's simple! The method is as follows: One part sugar to one part water.

Combine the sugar and water in a small saucepan over a medium heat and gently stir until the sugar dissolves. Leave to cool, then store in an airtight container for up to 2 weeks.

BROWN SUGAR SIMPLE SYRUP

Add 200g (7oz) of brown sugar to a small pan. Pour 240ml (8fl oz) of water into the pan. Heat this over medium heat, stirring occasionally until the sugar dissolves. Remove from the heat and let it cool. Store the syrup in an airtight container in the refrigerator for up to one week.

CONCORD GRAPE SYRUP

The sweetness inherent in grapes means no sugar need apply. Simply take 150g (5oz) rinsed Concord grapes (although any red or black grapes will do) and put them in a small saucepan. Cook over a medium heat, stirring, until the grape skins begin to break and the juice and flesh spill out into the pan. Cook down for about 5 minutes. Cool and press through a fine mesh sieve, discarding the extra pulp, skins and stems. Store in an airtight container for up to 2 weeks.

GINGER SYRUP

Add 200g (7oz) of sugar to a small pan. Add 1 thumb-sized piece of peeled and sliced ginger to the pan. Pour 240ml (8fl oz) of water into the pan. Heat this over medium heat, stirring occasionally until the sugar dissolves. Remove from the heat and let the ginger steep for 20 minutes. Strain out the ginger with a mesh strainer. Store the syrup in an airtight container in the refrigerator for up to one week.

HONEY-GINGER SYRUP

Add 240ml (8fl oz) honey to a small pan. Add 1 thumb-sized piece of peeled and sliced ginger to the pan. Pour 240ml (8fl oz) of water into the pan. Cook over high heat, stirring occasionally until the mixture boils. Reduce the heat to medium and simmer for 5 minutes. Remove from the heat and let the ginger steep for 20 minutes. Strain out the ginger with a mesh strainer. Store the syrup in an airtight container in the refrigerator for up to one week.

MINT SIMPLE SYRUP

200g (7oz) granulated white sugar
240ml (8fl oz) water
5g (⅛oz) fresh mint leaves, washed

Drop the mint into a small saucepan and gently muddle to release the oils. Add the sugar and water and cook over a medium heat. Gently stir until the sugar dissolves and the aroma of the mint is prominent. Leave to cool, then store in an airtight container for up to 2 weeks.

VARIATIONS

Basil Simple Syrup – make as above but use basil instead of mint.
Ginger Simple Syrup – cook the sugar and water as before and add a 125g (4oz) piece of ginger, peeled and very thinly sliced. Bring to a simmer, remove from the heat and leave to steep for 30 minutes. Pour through a fine-mesh sieve into an airtight container.
Honey Syrup – combine 240ml (8fl oz) honey with the water in a saucepan and continue as before.

Rosemary Syrup – make as the mint simple syrup (see page 11) but add 1 or 2 sprigs of rosemary.

Sage–Lime Syrup – make as the mint simple syrup (see page 11) but add a few sage leaves and the juice of 1 lime.

CITRUS-INFUSED VODKA

Use a combination of lemons, limes and oranges (1 of each fruit for an entire bottle works well) to create a custom blend. Rinse the fruit and cut into slices. Infuse for 3 days to a full week.

CLEMENTINE GIN (makes approximately 900ml/30fl oz)

3 large (or 5 small) clementines
200g (7oz) caster sugar
700ml (24fl oz) London dry gin

Quarter the clementines, keeping the skin on, and add them to a sterilised 1½ litre (50fl oz) jar. Add the sugar and gin, seal the jar and leave it to steep somewhere dark and dry for 2 weeks. Give the jar a shake every few days to help dissolve the sugar. After 2 weeks, strain through a sieve. Discard the clementines and pour the gin back into the jar or into a sterilised bottle. If you leave this gin for 3 weeks, the flavour of the pith will come through and it will have a more marmalady flavour. Don't steep it for longer than 3 weeks or it will become bitter.

SLOE GIN (makes approximately 850ml/28fl oz)

400g (14oz) sloes
2 almonds
125g (4½oz) caster sugar
700ml (24fl oz) London dry gin

Prepare your sloes by pricking them all over with a sterilised needle or putting them in a freezerproof tub or bag and freezing them for 48 hours to crack them. Tip the sloes into a 1½ litre (50fl oz) sterilised jar. Lightly crush the almonds and add them to the jar with the sugar. Pour in the gin. Seal the jar and leave it to steep somewhere dark and dry for 3–12 months. Shake the jar every few days during the first couple of weeks to help dissolve the sugar. After at least 3 months, strain the gin through a sieve and taste it. If it's too tart for your taste, stir in a little Simple Syrup (see page 9) until it's sweet enough. Pour back into the jar or a sterilised bottle.

WHITE PEACH PURÉE

450g (1lb) ripe white peaches, washed and
cut into quarters, stones discarded
30ml (1fl oz) freshly squeezed lemon juice
45ml (1½fl oz) Simple Syrup (see page 9)

Purée all the ingredients in a blender or food processor until very smooth. Freeze or store in the refrigerator in an airtight container for up to a week.

VARIATIONS

Really anything goes in terms of fruits, so try using your favourite and experiment.

Strawberry Purée – make as above but use 400g (14oz) washed, hulled and halved strawberries, 22ml (¾fl oz) freshly squeezed lemon juice and 30ml (1fl oz) Simple Syrup (see page 9).

Watermelon Purée – make as above but use 300g (10½oz) cubed watermelon, 15ml (½fl oz) freshly squeezed lemon or lime juice and 30ml (1fl oz) Simple Syrup (see page 9).

	Venetian Spritz	Fragola Spritz	Tiziano	Grand Avenue Frolic	Mimosa Sud	Rise of the Mojito	Fizzy Watermelon Margarita	Islay Sour	Sunday in the Park	Air Mail	How Blue Am I?	Kiwi Cooler	White Lady	Breakfast Martini	Espresso Martini	Tom Collins	Gin & Tonic	Negroni	Gin Rickey	Bees Knees	French 75	Gin Hot Toddy	Sloe Gin Fizz	Sloe Gin Sour	Classic Margarita	Frozen Margarita	Mezcalita
Gin												•	•	•	•	•	•	•	•	•	•	•	•	•			
Whisky/bourbon								•																			
Tequila/mezcal							•																		•	•	•
Rum						•				•																	
Vodka		•		•								•															
Cointreau (triple sec)				•					•				•	•											•	•	
Prosecco/ champagne	•	•	•	•	•	•	•	•	•	•	•	•									•						
Rosé																											
Aperol	•																										
Kahlua/Tia Maria															•												
Campari																		•									
Vermouth																		•									
Soda water	•															•			•				•				
Tonic water																	•										
Ginger beer																											
Ginger ale																											
Sparkling lemonade																											
Tomato juice																											
Cranberry juice				•																							
Espresso															•												
Chamomile tea									•																		
Jasmine tea																											
Strawberries		•																									
Lemon		•										•	•	•		•				•	•				•		
Lime				•		•	•			•			•							•					•	•	•
Orange				•	•				•					•				•		•		•					
Grapefruit								•																			
Clementine																						•		•			

	Tequila Mojito	La Cabrona	Lobo Negro	Paloma Classic	Pechuga Tonic	Pepe Collins	Old Fashioned	Manhattan	Whiskey Rickey	Penicillin	Kentucky Mule	Mint Julep	Bourbon Smash	Whisky Sour	Whisky Flip	Irish Coffee	Hot Toddy	London Fog	Rosé & Tonic	Rosé Mojito	Pink Wine Spritzer	Spicy Spritzer	Rosé Cosmo	Lavender Pink Lemonade	Frosé	Rosaquiri	Sweet Honey Rosé	Sage Gimlet	Rosé Collins	Jasmine Tea Tini
																												•		
							•	•	•	•	•	•	•	•	•	•	•	•									•		•
	•	•	•	•	•	•	•																			•				
																						•	•							•
																							•							
																			•	•	•	•	•	•	•	•	•	•	•	•
								•																						
	•			•			•	•												•	•									
					•													•												
										•																				
																						•								
																	•													
																							•							
																•	•													
																														•
																									•					
						•				•			•	•			•						•	•	•			•	•	•
		•	•	•				•				•								•						•		•	
		•					•															•	•						
				•																									

	Venetian Spritz	Fragola Spritz	Tiziano	Grand Avenue Frolic	Mimosa Sud	Rise of the Mojito	Fizzy Watermelon Margarita	Islay Sour	Sunday in the Park	Air Mail	How Blue Am I?	Kiwi Cooler	White Lady	Breakfast Martini	Espresso Martini	Tom Collins	Gin & Tonic	Negroni	Gin Rickey	Bees Knees	French 75	Gin Hot Toddy	Sloe Gin Fizz	Sloe Gin Sour	Classic Margarita	Frozen Margarita	Mezcalita
Sloes																							•	•			
Watermelon							•																				
Grapes			•																								
Blueberries																											
Kiwi												•															
Blackberries																											
Raspberries																											
Cucumber																											
Mint		•				•						•															
Ginger									•																		
Honey										•										•		•					
Cinnamon																						•					
Cloves																						•					
Basil											•																
Chillies																											
Lavender																											
Rosemary																											
Sage																											
Sugar																					•						
Egg													•											•			
Agave nectar																											•
Angostura bitters																											
Marmalade														•													
Horseradish																											
Tabasco sauce																											
Worcestershire sauce																											
Vanilla ice cream																											

Tequila Julep	Tequila Mojito	La Cabrona	Lobo Negro	Paloma Classic	Pechuga Tonic	Pepe Collins	Old Fashioned	Manhattan	Whiskey Rickey	Penicillin	Kentucky Mule	Mint Julep	Bourbon Smash	Whisky Sour	Whisky Flip	Irish Coffee	Hot Toddy	London Fog	Rosé & Tonic	Rosé Mojito	Pink Wine Spritzer	Spicy Spritzer	Rosé Cosmo	Lavender Pink Lemonade	Frosé	Rosaquiri	Sweet Honey Rosé	Sage Gimlet	Rosé Collins	Jasmine Tea Tini
			•																											
																													•	
•	•											•	•							•										
			•							•																				
										•							•											•		•
																	•													
																	•													
																						•								
																									•					
																										•				
																												•		
			•				•			•		•	•	•	•	•				•					•	•	•		•	•
														•	•															
•	•	•			•		•																							
								•	•																					
																		•												

VENETIAN SPRITZ

The first time I had this refreshing, super-easy aperitif was not, as the name might imply, in Venice. It was in Red Hook, Brooklyn, one of the earlier settlements in New York City's history as an American Revolution point of defence and, eventually, a bustling port. The bar where the Venetian Spritz first passed my lips is called Fort Defiance, named for the stalwart spot that defended the area during the Battle of Long Island. But there was no battle when I sipped this lovely pre-dinner quencher. Aperol is a bitter Italian liqueur, lower in alcohol and a little sweeter than its similarly red-hued cousin, Campari. For that reason, it makes a lovely complement to Prosecco's typical orchard fruitiness. A brut-style balances the Aperol nicely. The olive? I was dubious, too, the first time I had this cocktail. But there was something about the sweet and sour that appealed to my cocktail-subversive side. If you are not so keen, feel free to simply sip this as-is, or with an orange slice.

Ingredients
45ml (1½fl oz) Aperol
90ml (3fl oz) brut-style Prosecco
a splash of soda water
1 Cerignola olive, red or green – your choice (optional)

Instructions
Fill a double rocks glass with ice. Pour in the Aperol followed by the Prosecco. Give it a little stir. Top up with a splash of soda water and garnish with a Cerignola olive.

FRAGOLA FIZZ

The key to this drink is giving your strawberries a good mashing – because you'll be sipping it with a straw, you don't want any getting stuck on the way up, so make sure you get all those solid pieces beneath your muddler! The fruitiness natural to Prosecco takes all those delicious strawberry aromatics and flavours to another level.

Ingredients
4 medium (or 3 large) strawberries, quartered
15ml (½fl oz) Mint Simple Syrup (see page 11)
15ml (½fl oz) freshly squeezed lemon juice
30ml (1fl oz) vodka
90–120ml (3–4fl oz) brut-style Prosecco

Instructions
Drop the strawberries into a Collins glass, pour in the Mint Simple Syrup and muddle until very pulpy. Add the lemon juice and vodka. Fill with ice, top with the Prosecco and give it a little stir to evenly distribute the mashed-up berries. Finish with a straw.

TIZIANO

Invented in Venice, this sparkling cocktail uses muddled black grapes to create its colour (the inspiration for its name, the 16th-century painter Tiziano Vecellio, was fond of the purplish-red hue that the cocktail's main ingredient adds). Where I live, Concord grapes are prolific and easy to find in the late summer and early autumn, so I use them to make a syrup that adds a fun local twist to this Italian tipple (although any red or black grapes will do).

Ingredients
30ml (1fl oz) Concord Grape Syrup (see page 9)
90–120ml (3–4fl oz) brut-style Prosecco

Instructions
Pour the grape syrup into a flute. Top with the Prosecco.

GRAND AVENUE FROLIC

In the town I grew up in, there is an old hotel called the Chequit, that used to be the site of a great bar where lots and lots of merrymaking occurred on a nightly basis all summer long. It was the 80s. There was lots of neon, asymmetrical hair, Depeche Mode, dancing and drinking of bright, tropical, summery things, like the Madras – a particularly popular tipple among my friends and me. I abandoned it as years went on for less fruity, more 'serious' cocktails. But the thing is, who wants to be so serious when sipping cocktails? Especially bubbly ones. This souped-up Madras is even more delicious with a splash of extra-dry Prosecco. Viva la 80s.

Ingredients
45ml (1½fl oz) vodka
22ml (¾fl oz) cranberry juice
22ml (¾fl oz) freshly squeezed orange juice
30ml (1fl oz) freshly squeezed lime juice
15ml (½fl oz) Cointreau
90ml (3fl oz) extra dry-style Prosecco
a wide piece of lime peel, to garnish

Instructions
Fill a cocktail shaker with ice. Pour in the vodka, cranberry juice, orange and lime juices and Cointreau. Shake well and strain into an ice-filled Collins glass. Top with the Prosecco, garnish with the lime peel and pop in a straw.

BRUT

DOC
PROSECCO
ITALY

750ml   12%abv

MIMOSA SUD

Perhaps one of the easiest cocktails to throw together is that classic brunch staple, the Mimosa. Orange juice, sparkling, boom! You're done. But not only that, you've got something refreshing and festive that never fails to put a smile on everyone's face. Taking a little extra effort, though, in the form of squeezing some fresh juice, makes a world of difference. Here, I like to add a little Italian twist with fresh blood orange juice, for both its flavour and gorgeous colour, along with an extra dry-style Prosecco to add a nice, round fruitiness to the sparkle and pop.

Ingredients
60ml (2fl oz) freshly squeezed blood orange juice
90–120ml (3–4fl oz) brut-style Prosecco

Instructions
Pour the blood orange juice into a flute. Top with the Prosecco.

RISE OF THE MOJITO

Adding a little Prosecco in place of the usual soda water in a Mojito makes this perennial fun favourite even more refreshing (and aromatic!). Definitely veer towards a drier-style Prosecco with a little more minerality (think DOCG Valdobbiadene), as it livens up and plays well with all that fresh, fragrant mint.

Ingredients

7–8 fresh mint leaves, plus an extra sprig to garnish
22ml (¾fl oz) Simple Syrup (see page 9)
22ml (¾fl oz) freshly squeezed lime juice
60ml (2fl oz) white rum
90ml (3fl oz) extra dry-style Prosecco

Instructions

Drop the mint leaves into a cocktail shaker and top with the Simple Syrup. Muddle until the leaves release their natural oils and you start to smell all that nice minty freshness. Add in some ice. Pour in the lime juice and rum and shake well. Strain into an ice-filled Collins glass. Top with the Prosecco, garnish with the mint sprig and pop in a straw.

FIZZY WATERMELON MARGARITA

Watermelon has got to be one of the most thirst-quenching fruits in the entire world. And actually, its name is no accident: the brightly-hued fruit is 92% water. But I don't have to tell you that despite the water, it's not without flavour – and, in this case, flavour that gets wonderfully kicked up with a little extra dry-style Prosecco.

Ingredients
90ml (3fl oz) Watermelon Purée (see page 13)
30ml (1fl oz) silver tequila
15ml (½fl oz) triple sec
22ml (¾fl oz) freshly squeezed lime juice
15ml (½fl oz) Simple Syrup (see page 9)
60ml (2fl oz) extra dry-style Prosecco
3 frozen watermelon cubes, to garnish
a fresh mint sprig, to garnish

Instructions
Combine the Watermelon Purée, tequila, triple sec, lime juice and Simple Syrup in a shaker filled with ice. Shake well and strain into an ice-filled double rocks glass. Top with the Prosecco. Skewer the frozen watermelon cubes onto a single toothpick and garnish with this and the mint sprig.

ISLAY SOUR

One recent spring evening on an unseasonably hot day where I live in New York, I had some pink grapefruit sitting around in the refrigerator. I was trying to figure out what to make to go with some fish I had for dinner and considered putting the grapefruit on the grill – it caramelizes the sugars and makes a nice smoky-sweet accent. But then I got to thinking: wouldn't it be cool to make a refreshing drink that emulated that smoky grapefruit flavour using mezcal or Islay Scotch? The answer was yes, yes it was! The drink on its own is lovely, but add a splash of brut-style Prosecco, and the flavours are really lifted up. I prefer the single malt Uigeadail from the wonderful Ardbeg distillery in Islay here, because its strong smoke component is beautifully balanced by a rich, fruity characteristic in the malt.

Ingredients
30ml (1fl oz) Ardbeg 'Uigeadail' single malt Scotch
30ml (1fl oz) pink grapefruit juice
8ml (¼fl oz) Simple Syrup (see page 9)
30–60ml (1–2fl oz) brut-style Prosecco
a wide piece of pink grapefruit peel, to garnish

Instructions
Fill a cocktail shaker with ice cubes. Pour in the Scotch, grapefruit juice and Simple Syrup. Shake for 20 seconds. Strain slowly into an ice-filled double rocks glass. Top with the Prosecco and garnish with the grapefruit peel.

BUNNAHABHAIN

CAOL ILA

BRUICHLADDICH

BOWMORE

ARDMORE

ARDBEG
LAGAVULIN

LAPHROAIG

ISLAY
SOUR

SUNDAY IN THE PARK

The delicate, soft floral notes of chamomile combined with a brut-style Prosecco make such a lovely combo, all they really need are some subtle accents via a little Cointreau and a touch of ginger. Combine the first three ingredients in a chilled thermos, grab a bottle of Prosecco and bring this concoction to your next picnic in the park.

Ingredients
90ml (3fl oz) unsweetened chamomile tea
15ml (½fl oz) Cointreau
8ml (¼fl oz) Ginger Simple Syrup (see page 11)
90ml (3fl oz) extra dry-style Prosecco
a slice of fresh peach or orange, to garnish

Instructions
Fill a Collins glass with ice. Pour in the tea, Cointreau and Ginger Simple Syrup. Stir for a few seconds and top with the Prosecco. Pop in a straw and garnish with a thin slice of fresh peach or orange.

AIR MAIL

If you've never had the pleasure of flipping through
Esquire's *Handbook for Hosts* (first published in 1949;
revisited in 1977), you're in for a time-warp treat.
Not only is it chock-full of hostess-with-the-mostest
recipes, advice on equipment and a funny picture of
a naked lady, it also offers up coin tricks to entertain
your guests and drink recipes like this little gem.

Ingredients
60ml (2fl oz) golden rum
22ml (¾fl oz) freshly squeezed lime juice
15ml (½fl oz) Honey Syrup (see page 11)
90–120ml (3–4fl oz) brut-style Prosecco
a lime twist, to garnish

Instructions
Combine the rum, lime juice and Honey Syrup in an ice-
filled shaker. Shake well and strain into an ice-filled Collins
glass. Top with the Prosecco and garnish with a lime twist.

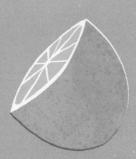

DON JUANCHO NIETO MELENDEZ
TEREPAIMA
VENEZUELA

AIR MAIL

RESERVA

70cl 40%

RUM

honey

HOW BLUE AM I?

I wrote my book, *Forager's Cocktails*, because I suspected that there were a lot of people like me out there: that is, folks who might be brave enough to pick up stinging nettles to see what they might inspire, but also those who really relish what to me is the kernel of the whole idea – using fresh, in-season items, be they from a woodland hike or a safari through your local farmer's market. You can forage for wild blueberries not too far from where I live, but you can also nab some pretty nice ones at the greengrocer. And picking off a handful of fresh basil leaves? Ahhh – such a beautiful scent and totally great combo with the fruit, lemon juice and Prosecco!

Ingredients

2oz (60g) fresh blueberries, plus 3–4 to garnish, rinsed
15ml (½fl oz) Basil Simple Syrup (see page 11)
45ml (1½fl oz) vodka
22ml (¾fl oz) freshly squeezed lemon juice
90ml (3fl oz) brut-style Prosecco

Instructions

Drop the blueberries into a shaker. Add the Simple Syrup and muddle thoroughly. Fill with ice, add the vodka and lemon juice and shake well. Strain through a fine mesh sieve into an ice-filled double rocks glass. Top with the Prosecco and garnish with the remaining blueberries.

KIWI COOLER

The soft, fleshy texture of kiwi fruit responds well to a little time in the freezer. Whiz it up with a gin like Hendrick's (with its pretty cucumber and floral notes) and a little mint simple syrup, top with a glug of extra dry-style Prosecco, and you have a super-chilly, sparkly cooler ripe for the quenching.

Ingredients
4 kiwi slices, just frozen (about 1 kiwi),
   plus 1 unfrozen slice to garnish
15ml (½fl oz) Mint Simple Syrup (see page 11)
8ml (¼fl oz) freshly squeezed lime juice
30ml (1fl oz) Hendrick's gin
60–90ml (2–3fl oz) extra dry-style Prosecco
a fresh mint sprig, to garnish

Instructions
Remove the kiwi slices from the freezer when they are just starting to harden. Drop in a blender or food processer with the Mint Syrup and lime juice, and blend until smooth. Strain through a fine-mesh sieve and pour into a tulip glass. Top with the Prosecco and garnish with a slice of kiwi and a mint sprig.

WHITE LADY

One of the greatest literary collaborations of the 20th century was not a book, but a cocktail. In the 1920s, Ernest Hemingway and F. Scott Fitzgerald both lived in Paris and, like all writers, they spent a lot of their time at the bar. At Harry's New York Bar (called that, even though it was in Paris), they found Harry MacElhone mixing drinks. Back in London, MacElhone had mixed crème de menthe, Cointreau and lemon juice together to make something like a White Lady. In Paris, with two infamous literary boozehounds making suggestions, he swapped the crème de menthe for gin. A few years later, back in London, The Savoy's bartender Harry Craddock added egg white to bring the drink together. It was named after Zelda Fitzgerald, a Jazz-Age It Girl and a platinum blonde.

Ingredients

45ml (1½fl oz) London dry gin
22ml (¾fl oz) Cointreau
22ml (¾fl oz) freshly squeezed lemon juice
15ml (½fl oz) Simple Syrup (see page 9)
15ml (½fl oz) egg white
a lemon twist, to garnish

Instructions

Pour the gin, Cointreau, lemon juice and Simple Syrup into an ice-filled cocktail shaker. Shake for 30 seconds to chill, then strain the liquid into a glass, discard the ice and add the cocktail mix back to the shaker. Pour in the egg white. Shake again for 30 seconds (this is called a reverse dry shake and ensures a fluffy finish). Strain into a chilled coupe glass and garnish with a lemon twist.

BREAKFAST MARTINI

The Breakfast Martini is the signature drink of London
bar scene supremo, Salvatore Calabrese. He invented
the Breakfast Martini in the 1990s, inspired by breakfast
with his wife Sue. Being Italian, Calabrese's preferred
breakfast is a shot of inky black espresso, but one morning
his wife persuaded him to sit down and eat breakfast
with her – tea, toast and marmalade. Inspired, he went
into work at the Library Bar in The Lanesborough Hotel
and mixed the first Breakfast Martini. I've swapped
in clementine gin to up the marmalade notes, but a
London dry or citrusy craft gin will work just as well.

Ingredients
50ml (1¾fl oz) Clementine Gin (see page 12)
15ml (½fl oz) triple sec
15ml (½fl oz) freshly squeezed lemon juice
1 heaped tsp orange marmalade
an orange twist, to garnish

Instructions
Pour all the ingredients into a shaker and stir well to dissolve
the marmalade. Add ice and give it a really good shake. Strain
into a chilled martini glass and garnish with an orange twist.

ESPRESSO MARTINI

In 1983, Dick Bradsell was mixing drinks at the Soho
Brasserie in London, when a famous model (Bradsell never
disclosed who) walked up to the bar and asked for a drink
that would 'wake me up, then **** me up'. Bradsell shook
a fresh espresso with vodka, Tia Maria, Kahlúa and sugar
syrup and strained it into a martini glass, calling it a Vodka
Espresso. Subsequently, he tweaked the recipe to perfect
his Espresso Martini and I've given it a go-over of my own,
swapping vodka for gin. The sweetness of Old Tom or the
clean sharpness of a jonge genever are good stand-ins
for vodka, and you can use either Tia Maria or Kahlúa or
a mix of both – I like Tia Maria for its darker, more bitter
coffee flavour. One essential is fresh espresso – the crema
on top of a freshly pulled shot of espresso helps create that
fluffy, creamy foam layer on top of the finished cocktail.
The usual garnish is three coffee beans, but I like a shake
of cocoa powder too for a faux cappuccino finish.

Ingredients

50ml (1¾fl oz) Old Tom gin or jonge genever
22ml (¾fl oz) Tia Maria or Kahlúa
22ml (¾fl oz) hot, fresh espresso
3 coffee beans and cocoa powder (optional), to garnish

Instructions

Half fill a cocktail shaker with ice and pour in the gin, Tia
Maria or Kahlúa and espresso. Shake together vigorously for
30 seconds, then strain into a chilled martini glass. Top with
3 coffee beans and a little dusting of cocoa powder, if using.

TOM COLLINS

'Have you seen Tom Collins?'
So went the opening line to a prank that took New York by storm in 1874. A man would tell his friend that a certain Tom Collins had been going about town spreading nasty lies about him, and that if he wanted to settle the matter, he would find Tom Collins in this or that bar. His friend would stomp off, outraged. But when he got to the distant bar, no Tom Collins could be found. That was, until an entrepreneurial bartender invented a drink called the Tom Collins. When furious men walked into his bar and demanded Tom Collins, he poured them the drink and charged them for it. That's one story anyway. John Collins, a barman working in London in the late 1880s, also claimed credit for the iconic recipe, as did a Mr Collins of the Whitehouse Tavern in 1870s New York, and as have many more Collinses the world over. That's the trouble with Tom Collins – you can never pin him down and find out the truth.

Ingredients
60ml (2fl oz) Old Tom gin
30ml (1fl oz) freshly squeezed lemon juice
15ml (½fl oz) Simple Syrup (see page 9)
120ml (4fl oz) soda water
an orange slice and a maraschino cherry, to garnish

Instructions
Pour the gin, lemon juice and Simple Syrup into an ice-filled cocktail shaker. Give it a vigorous shake. Fill a large highball glass with ice and strain the gin mix into it. Top up with soda water and garnish with an orange slice and a maraschino cherry.

GIN & TONIC

In the 1990s, bucking the vodka-cranberry trend, I drank
gin and tonic. Everybody laughed at this because G&Ts
were grandma drinks – dusty, fusty, old fashioned things.
In pubs there was only ever one choice of gin, and it was
meanly squirted into a stubby glass with a miserly rattle of
ice cubes and a thin, wizened slice of lemon. How things
have changed. Bars today line up rows of gem-coloured
bottles of gin and boast about their range. Bartenders tailor
the garnish to the gin, and you're as likely to get your G&T
in a goldfish-bowl-sized Spanish copa glass as a highball
with sturdy sides and branded etchings. My years of patiently
sipping G&Ts have finally been rewarded – hallelujah!
When it comes to making a G&T at home, use a roomy
glass and pack it with ice. The more ice, the slower it
melts and the less it dilutes your drink. I like a 1:2 ratio
of gin to tonic, so I can feel the gin's edge without
falling over it too quickly. And as for garnishes: the
world is your lemon. Pick something that chimes with
the botanicals in your gin to bring out the flavour.

Ingredients
60ml (2fl oz) gin
120ml (4fl oz) tonic water
to garnish: pick from lemon wedges, lime wedges,
   grapefruit wedges, cucumber twists, chilli slices, herb
   sprigs, juniper berries, coriander seeds, black peppercorns,
   cinnamon sticks, vanilla pods, lavender sprigs…

Instructions
Fill a highball or copa glass with ice and add your garnish,
then pour in the gin and top up with tonic water.

NEGRONI

I was introduced to the Negroni by my friend Sara Ross
on a trip to her family's home city of Genoa. It was my
first trip to Italy, and before taking us out to eat our body
weight in pasta, Sara told us it was important to warm
up with a Negroni. Ice cold, sharp and shocking, it's one
of the few drinks that really will perk up your taste buds
and get your stomach revved up, ready for dinner.
Making a good Negroni depends on the ingredients.
Campari is inevitable. The gin should be a strong London
dry gin – minimum 40% ABV so it has enough heft to grapple
with the flavours of the Campari and the vermouth. For
the sweet vermouth, I like Punt e Mes, which has notes of
dark chocolate mixed in with its weed-like tangle of herbal
bitters. For something a little lighter, try Cinzano Rosso.

Ingredients

22ml (¾fl oz) sweet vermouth
22ml (¾fl oz) Campari
22ml (¾fl oz) London dry gin
an orange slice, to garnish

Instructions

Fill an old fashioned glass with ice and pour in the
vermouth, then the Campari and then the gin. Briefly
stir, then tuck in a slice of orange and serve.

GIN RICKEY

Nowhere is summer hotter, stickier or muggier than in the swamps of Washington DC when there is an election campaign on. Back in 1883, after celebrating the election of his favourite candidate for House Speaker, Democratic lobbyist Colonel Joe Rickey walked into Shoomaker's bar and invented the Rickey. He instructed the bartender George Williamson to mix rye whiskey, lime juice and soda together to make a refreshing summer drink that was as good for hangovers as it was for thirst. The Colonel stayed true to rye, but the crowd at Shoomaker's liked gin better.

Ingredients
juice of 1 lime
60ml (2fl oz) gin
120ml (4fl oz) soda water
a lime wedge, to garnish

Instructions
Half fill a highball glass with ice and pour in the lime juice. Top up with gin and then soda water. Give it a brief stir, then drop in a lime wedge to garnish.

BEES KNEES

This is a Prohibition-era cocktail straight from the speakeasies of 1920s America. It's a kind of gin sour, but with honey syrup adding a balancing dash of sweetness instead of the usual sugar syrup. The honey and the citrus juices would also have helped make the bootleg gin taste a little nicer back in the '20s.

Ingredients
2 tsp runny honey
2 tsp hot water
45ml (1½fl oz) London dry gin
15ml (½fl oz) freshly squeezed lemon juice
15ml (½fl oz) freshly squeezed orange juice
an orange twist, to garnish

Instructions
Stir the honey and hot water together in a shaker to dissolve the honey. Fill the shaker with ice. Pour in the gin, lemon and orange juice. Shake together vigorously, then strain into a martini glass. Garnish with an orange twist.

CHAMPAGNE
2015
BRUT   12 5% vol
PRODUCT OF FRANCE

FRENCH 75

The Soixante-Quinze was a 75-millimetre light field gun used by the French army in the First World War. It was a powerful weapon, firing 15 rounds a minute, and is supposed to be the inspiration behind this crisp, fizzy cocktail. One legend has French troops sitting in their trenches with all the ingredients to mix the cocktail – including the Champagne – but no glasses, so they served them in empty 75mm shells. Except the first published recipe for the 75 doesn't include Champagne (or French soldiers living it up). Instead, it shakes up brandy, gin, grenadine and lemon juice. A few more evolutions occur until, in 1927, the familiar mix of gin, Champagne, lemon juice and sugar came together. Unlike the modern version of the drink, which is served in a flute, this 1920s French 75 is served in a tall glass over plenty of ice.

Ingredients

35ml (1 ¼fl oz) freshly squeezed lemon juice
3 tsp caster sugar
45ml (1 ½fl oz) London dry gin
90ml (3fl oz) brut Champagne
a lemon slice, to garnish

Instructions

Stir the lemon juice and sugar together in a cocktail shaker until the sugar dissolves. Add ice and the gin and shake together well. Fill a tall glass with ice and strain in the gin mix. Top up with Champagne and garnish with a slice of lemon.

GIN HOT TODDY

Good news! There is a cure for the common cold, and its name is gin. Not that you can apply gin to your cold in any old fashion and expect your symptoms to clear up. You have to do it in the right way. You have to do it in a hot toddy. Whenever I start to feel the cotton wool fogginess of a cold descending, I prescribe myself two Gin Hot Toddies before bed (never more nor less). In the morning I wake up free from coughs, sneezes, sniffles and soreness and I'm grateful to gin all over again.

Ingredients
35ml (1¼fl oz) Clementine Gin (see page 12)
juice of 1 clementine
1 tsp runny honey
1 cinnamon stick
4 cloves
1 orange slice
150ml (5fl oz) hot water

Instructions
Pour the gin and clementine juice into a heatproof glass or mug. Stir in the honey to dissolve it. Drop in the cinnamon stick. Stick the cloves into the orange slice and drop it into the mug. Top up with just boiled hot water, stirring a few times with the cinnamon stick to mix, and then serve.

SLOE GIN FIZZ

A classic mid-19th-century cocktail, the Gin Fizz comes in many guises. There are Silver Fizzes with added egg white, Royal Fizzes with whole eggs mixed in, the famous Ramos Gin Fizz, which features cream, orange flower water and lime juice amongst its ingredients, and then there is this pale purple Sloe Gin Fizz, which swaps dry gin for sweet, hedgerow-scented sloe gin. A tall sour, it's a great summer cocktail.

Ingredients
60ml (2fl oz) Sloe Gin (see page 12)
30ml (1fl oz) freshly squeezed lemon juice
8ml (¼fl oz) Simple Syrup (see page 9)
soda water, to top up
a lemon wedge and a mint sprig, to garnish

Instructions
Pour the Sloe Gin, lemon juice and Simple Syrup into an ice-filled cocktail shaker. Shake together well. Fill a tall glass with ice, strain in the gin mix, then top up with soda water for the fizz. Garnish with a wedge of lemon and a sprig of fresh mint.

SLOE GIN SOUR

I'm going to describe this as a very Christmassy drink. Not that you should limit yourself to drinking it at Christmas. In fact, the bright citrusy flavours would be delightful on any sunny afternoon. But it's the combination of sloes and clementines in it that makes me think of dark December days, twinkling lights, tinsel and mistletoe. And also how it looks in the glass: a royal purple drink with a layer of snowy white foam on top. There's something very celebratory about it that somehow, I reckon, it could turn any event into the most wonderful day of the year.

Ingredients
45ml (1 ½fl oz) Sloe Gin (see page 12)
15ml (½fl oz) Clementine Gin (see page 12)
15ml (½fl oz) freshly squeezed lemon juice
15ml (½fl oz) egg white
an orange twist, to garnish

Instructions
Pour the Sloe Gin, Clementine Gin and lemon juice into a cocktail shaker. Add ice and shake vigorously for 30 seconds, then strain into a glass. Discard the ice and pour the cocktail back into the shaker along with the egg white. Shake again for 30 seconds. Strain into a chilled coupe glass and garnish with an orange twist.

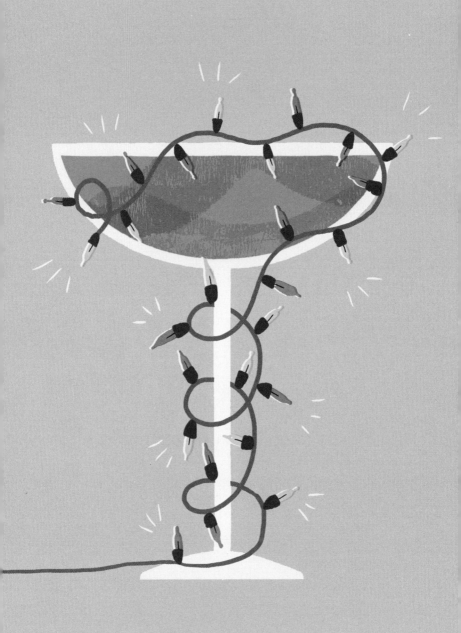

CLASSIC MARGARITA

Quite possibly named after a beautiful woman, the Margarita is believed to be the Mexican version of a traditional Daisy. The Daisy is a cocktail that combines a shot of liquor, lemon juice and orange cordial. Regardless of how the Margarita came to be, its foolproof recipe and balanced flavour with sweet, savoury and tart notes has made it not only the quintessential tequila cocktail, but also one of the most popular cocktails in history.

Ingredients
30ml (1fl oz) freshly squeezed lime juice, plus extra for the rim
60ml (2fl oz) tequila (blanco or reposado)
30ml (1fl oz) Cointreau
salt, for the rim

Instructions
Moisten the rim of an old fashioned glass with water or lime juice and, holding it upside down, dip the rim into a flat dish filled with table or kosher salt. Place the tequila, Cointreau and lime juice in a cocktail shaker filled with ice. Shake and strain the drink into the prepared glass filled with ice cubes and serve.

FROZEN MARGARITA
(Serves 4)

At the height of tequila's popularity in the 1970s, the slushy, frozen version of the Margarita was popular all over the US. It was in 1971 that a young Mexican-American with the dream of becoming a successful restaurateur was struggling to expedite an array of blended frozen Margaritas to his clientele. Then Mariano Martinez had a revelation. After a trip to the local 7-Eleven store, he saw a Slurpee frozen drinks machine and knew what he had to do. Unable to acquire such a machine, Martinez adapted an old soft-serve ice-cream machine to streamline the production of what has become one of the world's favourite frozen alcoholic beverages. To this day, Martinez's iconic invention sits at the Smithsonian's National Museum of American History.

Ingredients
240ml (8fl oz) freshly squeezed lime juice, plus extra for the rim
240ml (8fl oz) blanco tequila
120ml (4fl oz) triple sec (preferably Cointreau)
4 cups of ice
salt, for the rim (optional)
lime wheels or wedges, to garnish

Instructions
Moisten the rim of a classic margarita glass with water or lime juice and, holding it upside down, dip the rim into a flat dish filled with table or kosher salt, if using. Place all the remaining ingredients, except the garnish, in a blender. Blend until slushy throughout and add more ice if necessary (if the consistency is more liquid than slush). Pour the drink into the prepared glass and garnish with lime wheels or wedges.

MEZCALITA

When it comes to the incredible range of Margarita variations, there is one version that simply cannot go unnoticed. It is also the simplest. The Mezcalita, or Mezcal Margarita, tastes exactly as it sounds – a smokier, more rugged version of the popular classic. Made with mezcal instead of tequila, the sweet citric notes of the espadín mezcal complement the delicious caramel agave notes of the agave nectar, creating an earthier and bolder flavour profile. Taming the smokiness with a bit of lime, the Mezcalita is the perfect way to introduce mezcal to any novices, who haven't yet decided to make the mezcal leap. Don't forget to add a bit of fiery sal de gusano, made with crushed agave worms, to the rim of the glass for extra kick.

Ingredients
30ml (1fl oz) freshly squeezed lime juice, plus extra for the rim
60ml (2fl oz) espadín mezcal
30ml (1fl oz) agave nectar
sal de gusano (see Note below) or regular salt, for the rim

Instructions
Moisten the rim of a martini glass with water or lime juice and, holding it upside down, dip the rim into a flat dish filled with the sal de gusano. Place all the remaining ingredients in a cocktail shaker filled with ice and shake well. Fine strain into the prepared glass and serve.

Note: Vegans and vegetarians be warned. Sal de gusano is made of crushed agave worms, chilli and salt.

STRAWBERRY MARGARITA SPRITZ

By now you've probably realised that there are infinite variations to what a Margarita can become. Three basic ingredients will define her: agave, a sweet liqueur and tart citrus. But what happens when you add a touch of Champagne to instantly elevate the occasion? The result is a sweet and fizzy Margarita that will make any given moment feel like Sunday brunch.

Ingredients
30ml (1fl oz) freshly squeezed lime juice, plus extra for the rim
45ml (1½fl oz) blanco tequila
30ml (1fl oz) fresh strawberry purée
1 teaspoon agave nectar
Champagne, to top up
salt, for the rim

Instructions
Moisten the rim of a coupe glass with water or lime juice. Holding the glass upside down, dip the rim into a flat dish filled with table or kosher salt. Place all the remaining ingredients, except the Champagne, in a cocktail shaker filled with ice and shake well. Strain into the prepared glass and top up with Champagne to serve.

BLOODY MARIA

The Bloody Mary was created in the 1920s by Fernand Petiot, at Harry's New York Bar in Paris, where American expatriates and artists such as Ernest Hemingway and Salvador Dali would frequently indulge in libations during the *années follies* (crazy years). The first version of this drink was made out of equal parts tomato juice and vodka, which had just arrived in the city alongside caviar and a population of refugees escaping the Russian Revolution. It is said to have been christened by two bar patrons from Chicago, who knew of a bar called Bucket of Blood, where there was a waitress named Mary. After taking the drink to the US, Petiot added spices, Worcestershire sauce and Tabasco to the mix. The drink's Mexican counterpart, the Bloody Maria, is made with tequila and is as legitimate as the original, adding a bit more character and vegetal earthiness to the mix, making it the perfect brunch drink.

Ingredients
60ml (2fl oz) reposado tequila
1 teaspoon drained bottled grated horseradish
3 dashes of Tabasco sauce
3 dashes of Worcestershire sauce
a dash of lime juice
3 dashes of salt
3 dashes of freshly ground black pepper
150ml (5fl oz) tomato juice
a lime wedge and a celery stalk, to garnish

Instructions
Mix all the ingredients, except the tomato juice and garnish, in a collins glass over ice and stir well. Top up with the tomato juice and stir again. Garnish with a lime wedge and a celery stalk and serve.

75

TEQUILA JULEP

Amid a celebration of Southern pride, over 120,000 Bourbon Mint Juleps are made during the annual Kentucky Derby, served to horse aficionados in traditional pewter cups overfilled with crushed ice as the staple of the world-famous race. The word 'julep' is derived from the Persian *gulab*, denoting sweetened rose water. The word crossed over to Arabic as *julab* and later *julapium* in Latin. Eventually, a julep came to be known as a medicinal syrup, flavoured with herbal essences. Before the Mint Julep became the favourite cocktail of the South, it was seen as a restorative tonic that would invigorate farmers before they would step out into the fields each morning. This julep, made with aged tequila and served in a copper mug, is a south-of-the-border version perfect for any warm summer evening.

Ingredients
5 mint sprigs
22ml (¾fl oz) agave nectar
60ml (2fl oz) añejo tequila

Instructions
Muddle 4 of the mint sprigs in the bottom of a julep cup (a copper or pewter mug is recommended). Add the agave nectar and a bar spoon of water. Fill the cup with crushed ice. Add the tequila and stir well. Garnish with the remaining mint sprig.

TEQUILA MOJITO

Originating in Cuba, the traditional Mojito was a humble attempt to mask the funky fierceness of cheap rum to make it more pleasing to the palate. And the mixture of lime, sugar and mint makes for an addictive combination. Legend has it that Ernest Hemingway would drink his Mojitos with Champagne instead of soda water at the iconic Havana bar, La Bodeguita del Medio. We can only imagine what he would have thought of switching his rum for tequila. For mint-lovers and Margarita-lovers alike, the Tequila Mojito is the dream, bringing together two of the world's favourite cocktails into a mouthwatering pairing.

Ingredients
4 mint leaves
30ml (1fl oz) agave nectar
30ml (1fl oz) freshly squeezed lime juice
60ml (2fl oz) Herradura Blanco tequila
60ml (2fl oz) soda water

Instructions
Place the mint leaves, agave nectar and lime juice in a collins glass. Mash the ingredients with a muddler or with the back of a spoon at the bottom of the glass. Next, fill the glass with ice cubes and add the tequila and soda water. Stir to blend.

LA CABRONA

Known as *La Doña*, María Félix remains a symbol of beauty, glamour, boldness and independence. Her beautiful features captivated an entire generation during the Golden Age of Mexican cinema; however, her outspoken views and strong character have immortalised her as a fiercely bold and ambitious woman, despite living and working in an era dominated by men. Her *cabrona* (badass) attitude carved her place as an icon for women in Mexico and around the world. This cocktail is inspired by her legacy.

Ingredients
22ml (¾fl oz) freshly squeezed lime juice, plus extra for the rim
45ml (1½fl oz) espadín mezcal
22ml (¾fl oz) freshly squeezed blood orange juice
15ml (½fl oz) agave nectar
hibiscus salt, for the rim

Instructions
Moisten the rim of an old fashioned glass with water or lime juice. Holding the glass upside down, dip the rim into the hibiscus salt. Place all the liquid ingredients in a cocktail shaker with ice and shake. Strain into the prepared glass over a large block of fresh ice.

LOBO NEGRO

The wolf is a symbol of the night. The often-misunderstood wolf is a fiercely loyal animal who, much like mezcal, is an undeterred free spirit. As a spirit animal, the lonesome wolf teaches us to take risks and discover our inner power and strength. The Lobo Negro cocktail, named after the rare black wolf, invites you to embrace your inner spirit animal. The smoky mezcal, combined with the spicy ginger syrup, brings out the sweet and earthy undertones of the blackberries for a cocktail that is not only delicious, but is also packed with antioxidants.

Ingredients
7 blackberries
60ml (2fl oz) Montelobos mezcal
45ml (1½fl oz) Ginger Syrup (see page 11)
30ml (1fl oz) freshly squeezed lime juice

Instructions
Place 4 of the blackberries in a cocktail shaker and muddle. Add the rest of the ingredients to the shaker, add ice, and shake well to mix. Strain into an old fashioned glass filled with fresh ice. Garnish with the remaining blackberries on a cocktail stick.

PALOMA CLASSIC

Possibly the most popular tequila cocktail in Mexico, the history of the refreshing and tasty Paloma can be traced back to one of the oldest bars in the country, situated in the small town of Jalisco that gave its name to this fiery spirit. If you haven't yet heard of La Capilla, just a sip of this drink and you may find yourself booking the first flight there! Picture a small, humble cantina on the corner of a cobbled street, where celebrities, rock stars and tequila aficionados flock from all corners of the world to try Don Javier Delgado Corona's cocktails, which include the classic Paloma, as well as a Coca-Cola, tequila and lime highball known as the Batanga. If you're lucky enough, the iconic Don Javier (now in his 90s) might even serve you himself. This delicious mixture of bitter grapefruit juice with lime, salt and tequila will awaken your senses and leave you asking for more.

Ingredients
60ml (2fl oz) blanco tequila
30ml (1fl oz) freshly squeezed grapefruit juice
15ml (½fl oz) freshly squeezed lime juice
a pinch of salt
1 tablespoon agave nectar
soda water, to top up
a grapefruit wedge or lime wedge, to garnish

Instructions
Mix all the ingredients, except the soda water and garnish, in a cocktail shaker filled with ice and shake for 15 seconds. Fill a collins glass with fresh ice cubes and strain the drink into the glass. Top up with soda water and stir briefly. Garnish with a grapefruit or lime wedge to serve.

PECHUGA TONIC

It's the beginning of spring, and with longer days, sunshine and new blooms comes the promise of thirst-quenching boozy tonics. The ever-so-popular Gin and Tonic gets revamped in this celebratory version with Pechuga mezcal. The history of the Mezcal de Pechuga in Santiago Matatlan can be traced back to 1930, when a stranger from Rio Seco migrated to the town. It is said that when a group of musicians came to the village, he held a reception in their honour and handed the leader a bottle of Pechuga. Many imbibed the spirit for the first time and, captivated by its sophisticated and unique flavours, it soon became the spirit of choice for celebratory occasions. The distillation of espadín mezcal with tropical fruits and spices, including tejocote, guava, pineapple, apples, cinnamon and clove, turns this particular mezcal into the perfect gin substitute. Add a sprig of thyme, or a peel of grapefruit or kaffir lime, and serve it in a big stemmed wine goblet, transforming your Pechuga Tonic into the perfect spring drink.

Ingredients
120ml (4fl oz) Fever Tree tonic water
60ml (2fl oz) Pechuga mezcal
1 slice of grapefruit or kaffir lime, to garnish
salt

Instructions
Pour the tonic water and mezcal into a stemmed wine goblet filled with ice and stir. Garnish with a grapefruit or lime slice and dust the top of the cocktail lightly with kosher salt.

PEPE COLLINS

The traditional Collins cocktail is that all-round good guy who fits every occasion. An everyday sipper and easy to make at the drop of a hat, the Pepe is the Mexican cousin of the John Collins, and is as refreshing as it is tasty. But as simple as it is to make, quality is key. Be sure to use your favourite tequila and not to skimp on quality, as it will be the star of the show in this icy cocktail, sure to become your new go-to drink.

Ingredients

45ml (1½fl oz) reposado tequila
30ml (1fl oz) freshly squeezed lemon juice
15ml (½fl oz) agave nectar
60ml (2fl oz) soda water
a lemon wedge, to garnish

Instructions

Pour the tequila, lemon juice and agave nectar into a collins glass filled with ice cubes. Stir thoroughly. Top with the soda water and garnish with a lemon wedge.

OLD FASHIONED

This drink is just that, old-fashioned. When celebrity bartender 'Professor' Jerry Thomas wrote the world's first bartenders' guide, *How to Mix Drinks or The Bon Vivant's Companion*, in 1862, his Old Fashioned recipe called for Holland Gin. By the 1880s, a bartender in Louisville, Kentucky, at the famed Pendennis Club, is believed to have popularised a bourbon version, taking it to New York's Waldorf Astoria Hotel, from where it spread to the rest of the world. Whatever its history, this is one of the most important whisky drinks around. We offer it both ways – the traditional recipe, and the modern, post-Prohibition version with muddled fruit. Both have their adherents, so why not try them both?

Ingredients

CLASSIC

60ml (2fl oz) good bourbon or rye whiskey
15ml (½fl oz) Simple Syrup (see page 9)
4 dashes of Angostura bitters
a large orange twist and an amarena cherry, to garnish

MODERN

1 sugar cube
6 dashes of Angostura bitters
a large orange twist and an amarena cherry
60ml (2fl oz) whiskey
60ml (2fl oz) soda water

Instructions

For the Classic, pour the whiskey into a glass named, appropriately enough, an old fashioned. Add the Simple Syrup and bitters. Add ice – preferably a single large cube or rock, but the larger the lumps the better. Cut a large orange twist, being careful to only get the skin and not the bitter pith, and express it over the drink with a twisting motion. Drop it in. Garnish with the orange twist and an amarena cherry. For the modern take, place a sugar cube in the glass and sprinkle it with the bitters. Add the orange twist and an amarena cherry and muddle the fruit and sugar cube. Pour in the whiskey and add ice, then top up with soda water. Serve.

MANHATTAN

Not only one of the finest cocktails ever served, this is also one of the most famous. Like many cocktails, the origins of the Manhattan are murky, although some say that it was created in the 1880s at the Manhattan Club for Winston Churchill's mother, Lady Randolph Churchill. This classic combination of whiskey, vermouth and bitters makes it a foundational cocktail for all bartenders, and a great drink for experimenting with different whiskies. Originally rye would have been used, but now bourbon and other whiskies appear in this drink in bars across the globe. Take it a step further and substitute dry vermouth for sweet for a 'Dry Manhattan', or use equal parts sweet and dry vermouth for a 'Perfect Manhattan'. One variation pays tribute to the legendary group of entertainers who put Las Vegas on the map. The 'Rat Pack Manhattan' has one ingredient for each member of the group, so in addition to the whiskey, use equal parts sweet and dry vermouth, a dash of Grand Marnier and 2 or 3 dashes of Angostura bitters. Stir over ice to the sounds of Sammy Davis Jr. and garnish with a cherry, and even an orange twist.

Ingredients
60ml (2fl oz) whiskey (bourbon or rye are most frequently used, or use Canadian whisky or a blended whisky)
30ml (1fl oz) good sweet vermouth
2 dashes of Angostura bitters
an amarena cherry, to garnish

Instructions
Into a cocktail mixing glass, pour the whiskey, sweet vermouth and bitters. Add some ice and stir with a barspoon until chilled – about 1 minute. Strain into a chilled martini glass and garnish with an amarena cherry.

WELCOME TO
Manhattan

HOTEL

Blanton's
THE ORIGINAL
SINGLE BARREL
BOURBON WHISKEY

Bourbon Whiskey dumped on 4-2009   from Barrel No 300
Stored in Warehouse   H   on Rick No 38
Traditionally selected filtered and bottled by hand at 93 Proof
RAIGHT BOURBON WHISKEY   46% ALC/VOL (93 PROOF)

WHISKEY RICKEY

This is a refreshing long drink that eschews sugar for
a tart combination of whiskey, lime and soda water.
This drink was originally created by a bartender
named George A. Williamson at Shoomaker's Bar in
Washington, D.C., in the 1880s. The original recipe calls
for bourbon, although any whisky (or preferably whiskey)
will work well in this drink. Ironically, it wasn't until gin
was substituted for bourbon about 10 years after this
drink's creation that the Rickey took off in popularity.
The large majority of Rickeys are still ordered with gin,
but try this with your favourite whiskey and enjoy a tipple
that 19th-century US Congressmen would have sipped
during the warm-weather months in the US capital.

Ingredients
60ml (2fl oz) bourbon or whiskey of choice
soda water, to top up
½ lime, for squeezing and garnish

Instructions
Fill a highball glass with ice, add the whiskey and top up with
soda water. Squeeze the ½ lime into the drink and drop in the
lime shell as a garnish.

PENICILLIN

The aptly named Penicillin is a modern classic crafted by bartender Sam Ross. Created in 2005, the Penicillin mixes Scotch whisky with honey, ginger and lemon to create one of the best and most popular Scotch-based drinks of modern times. Walk into a mixology bar in Hong Kong, London, Seattle or anywhere in between, sidle up to the bar and order a Penicillin and enjoy the drink that has gone viral.

Ingredients

60ml (2fl oz) blended Scotch whisky
22ml (¾fl oz) Honey-Ginger Syrup (see page 11)
22ml (¾fl oz) freshly squeezed lemon juice
8ml (¼fl oz) Islay single malt Scotch whisky
grated candied ginger, to garnish

Instructions

Pour the blended Scotch whisky, Honey-Ginger Syrup, lemon juice and Islay whisky into a mixing glass. Add some ice and stir for 1 minute. Strain into a chilled coupe glass and garnish with a little candied ginger on a cocktail pick.

KENTUCKY MULE

This cocktail is a member of the family of drinks known as mules or bucks, of which the most famous is the vodka-based Moscow Mule, created in the 1940s at Hollywood's famous Cock 'n' Bull. However, mules and bucks have been around for much longer. While the origin of these drinks is unclear, legend has it that adding a spirit such as whisky to ginger beer gave the drink a 'kick', hence the name. Obviously, bourbon is the classic call here, but rye whiskey will up the spiciness factor a bit, while an American blended whiskey is a perfectly fine choice for a lighter, smoother option. The choice is yours.

Ingredients
60ml (2fl oz) bourbon
120ml (4fl oz) ginger beer
a lime wedge, to garnish

Instructions
Pour the bourbon into a copper mug. Add fresh ice cubes, then fill to the brim with ginger beer. Garnish with a lime wedge.

MINT JULEP

A symbol of the American South, the Mint Julep is inextricably linked to the Kentucky Derby horse race, where it has been the official drink since 1938. Amazingly, up to 120,000 juleps are consumed at Churchill Downs over Derby weekend every year. The word 'julep' is descended from the Arabic drink 'julab', which is made with water and rose petals. The modern julep dates back to the 1700s, and the silver or pewter julep cup is key to this drink. Glass is an insulator, so a proper julep cup will get icy on the outside while it sits. Spearmint is the go-to mint in the South, although peppermint will also work in a pinch. The julep is a rare drink that actually gets better as it sits, so try your hand at one of these on a warm summer day, then sit back and relax, sipping slowly as the world whizzes by.

Ingredients
a large bunch of mint sprigs
15ml (½fl oz) Simple Syrup (see page 9)
60ml (2fl oz) bourbon

Instructions
In the bottom of a julep cup, add 8–10 mint leaves, stripped from the bunch, and half the Simple Syrup. Gently muddle the mint in the Simple Syrup, being careful not to bruise the leaves. Fill the julep cup with crushed ice, mounding it over the top and creating a look reminiscent of a snow cone. Slowly pour the bourbon over the top of the ice, followed by the remaining Simple Syrup. Next, take the remaining bunch of mint sprigs and give them a good spank between your hands to release the essential oils. Place these into the ice as a garnish, along with a short (paper) straw so that the aromas of the drink can be better enjoyed.

BOURBON SMASH

A close cousin of the Mint Julep, the Bourbon Smash is
enhanced with a slightly different preparation and the
addition of lemon juice. The resulting cocktail combines the
mint of a julep with the lemon of a sour, creating a happy
medium of both. This cocktail takes well to freshly muddled
fruit (think berries in particular) as an additional alternative.
The smash is a drink that deserves more attention than it
currently gets and is perfect as a warm-weather cocktail.

Ingredients
8–10 mint leaves, plus a sprig to garnish
15ml (½fl oz) Simple Syrup (see page 9)
60ml (2fl oz) bourbon
22ml (¾fl oz) freshly squeezed lemon juice

Instructions
Place the mint leaves at the bottom of a cocktail shaker. Add
the Simple Syrup and gently muddle the mint leaves. Add some
ice cubes, and pour in the bourbon and lemon juice. Shake
vigorously and strain into an old fashioned glass filled with
fresh ice cubes. Garnish with a sprig of freshly spanked mint.

WHISKY SOUR

This is a simple but delectable combination of whisky, lemon juice, sugar and, optionally, egg white. The egg white gives a richer mouthfeel, but either way this drink is a classic not to be missed. The Whisky Sour is another foundational drink that allows the mixer to create some fun variations. Why not try adding a barspoon of good British orange marmalade to the cocktail shaker for an interesting twist? Traditionally, this drink would be made with bourbon, but feel free to use whatever whisky you prefer. Irish whiskey and Canadian whisky would be great choices here, and a Japanese blended whisky could work well.

Ingredients
45ml (1½fl oz) whisky
22ml (¾fl oz) freshly squeezed lemon juice
22ml (¾fl oz) Simple Syrup (see page 9)
1 egg white (optional)
a lemon wheel and an amarena cherry, to garnish

Instructions
Pour the whisky, lemon juice, Simple Syrup and separated egg white, if using, into a cocktail shaker. Add some ice and shake vigorously for 1 minute. Strain into an old fashioned glass filled with fresh ice cubes. Garnish with a lemon wheel and an amarena cherry.

BRUICHLA

PROGRESSIVE HEBRIDEAN
DISTILLERS

BRUICHLADDICH

THE
CLASSIC
LADDIE
SCOTTISH BARLEY

IT IS OUR MISSION TO
PURSUE THE ULTIMATE
PEDIGREE, PROVENANCE
AND TRACEABILITY OF
OUR RAW MATERIALS.
CHIEF OF WHICH IS OUR
BARLEY. AND TO PUSH
THE BOUNDARIES OF THE
CONCEPT OF TERROIR IN
ARTISANAL SINGLE
MALT WHISKY.

UNPEATED
ISLAY SINGLE MALT
SCOTCH WHISKY

DISTILLED, MATURED AND BOTTLED
UN-CHILL FILTERED AND COLOURING-FREE
AT BRUICHLADDICH DISTILLERY,
ISLE OF ISLAY, SCOTLAND.
PRODUCT OF SCOTLAND.

750 ML
50% ALC/VOL.

WHISKY FLIP

This is about as old school as cocktails get. Whisky, egg and sugar, shaken together into a froth that is far more than the sum of its parts. The flip is a great drink to have in your repertoire, as it's anything but run of the mill, has a long history and, most importantly, tastes great. In 1695, 'flip' was originally used for a mixture of rum, beer and sugar that was heated with a red-hot iron, or loggerhead. The intense heat of the iron caused the drink to froth up or 'flip', hence the name. Over time, beer was replaced with whisky, more sugar was added, an egg found its way into the mix, and the drink stopped being served hot. This recipe is for the 1800s-era version of the 'flip', and is easily the most suited for a modern palate.

Ingredients
60ml (2fl oz) whisky
30ml (1fl oz) Simple Syrup (see page 9)
1 whole egg
1 nutmeg, for grating, to garnish

Instructions
Put the whisky and Simple Syrup into a cocktail shaker, then crack in the whole egg. Add some ice and shake hard for 60 seconds. Strain into a wine glass and grate some nutmeg over the top.

IRISH COFFEE

This cocktail can trace its origin back to Shannon Airport in the 1950s, where it was first created by Joe Sheridan to warm up a group of cold and travel-weary American travellers. Back home, two San Franciscans, writer Stanton Delaplane and Jack Koeppler – the owner of a local bar, called the Buena Vista – set out to recreate the drink they had first tasted back in Shannon. Eventually, the two men hit on the perfect combination of coffee, sugar, Irish whiskey (no substitutions, please!) and whipped cream. The drink became such a hit at the Buena Vista (which serves up to 2,000 Irish coffees a day) that this increase in demand eventually helped to revive the flagging fortunes of the Irish whiskey industry. All from one little drink. So while you sip, take a moment to reflect on how two friends half a world away may have inadvertently saved the Irish whiskey industry and raise a toast to Misters Delaplane and Koeppler.

Ingredients

45ml (1½fl oz) Irish whiskey
15ml (½fl oz) Brown Sugar Simple Syrup (see page 9)
120ml (4fl oz) freshly brewed black coffee
whipped cream, to garnish

Instructions

Into a heatproof mug, pour the Irish whiskey and Simple Syrup. Top with the freshly brewed coffee. Then, using a barspoon, carefully pour whipped cream off the back of the spoon onto the surface of the coffee so that the cream floats. Serve hot.

IRISH
COFFEE

IRISH WHISKEY
DUBLIN
ROE & CO

BLENDED IRISH WHISKEY

PRODUCT OF IRELAND

BATCH 3 : BOTTLE NO. 1236

70cl 45%abv

KENTUCKY STRAIGHT

BOURBON
WHISKEY
AGED 20 YEARS

700ml 90.2PROOF

ARTISAN
HONEY

HOT TODDY

This is a drink that has been used to take the chill off one's bones and to cure what ails since perhaps the very creation of whisky itself. It is the kind of drink that would have been served in 18th-century taverns and inns across Scotland, with the mugful of water heated by a large piece of iron called a loggerhead, which was kept in the fireplace just for the purpose. But don't let its simplicity fool you – this drink is far more than the single ingredients. Once you've mastered the toddy, feel free to play around with variations. You can easily substitute the hot water for your favourite tea (I recommend Earl Grey) or switch the honey for another sweetener.

Ingredients

30ml (1fl oz) honey
15ml (½fl oz) freshly squeezed lemon juice
45ml (1½fl oz) whisky
60ml (2fl oz) hot water
a cinnamon stick, to garnish
½ lemon wheel studded with cloves, to garnish

Instructions

Into a heatproof glass mug, pour the honey, lemon juice and whisky. Add the hot water and stir to combine. Garnish with a cinnamon stick and the half lemon wheel studded with cloves. Serve hot.

LONDON FOG

(Serves 24 120-ml/4-oz servings)

This classic yet simple ice-cream-based drink is perfect for parties. All you need is a punch bowl, some vanilla ice cream and coffee (cold-brew works best, but don't let it prevent you from making this if you don't have any around), decent whiskey and a ladle. Questions about the origin of this drink abound, but many credit computer programmer Ward Cunningham, developer of the world's first wiki, for popularising the drink by serving it as his signature cocktail at holiday gatherings. No matter how it came about, this is a great party drink that is certain to impress a crowd.

Ingredients

2 litres (½ gallon) drippy vanilla ice cream (leave out of the freezer for at least 35 minutes)
475ml (16fl oz) bourbon
475ml (16fl oz) cold-brewed coffee

Instructions

Combine the ice cream, bourbon and coffee in a punch bowl. Stir occasionally as the ice cream melts. Serve in punch cups. This cocktail is to be drunk, but a spoon can also be used.

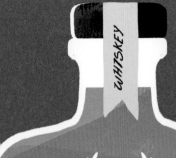

WHISKEY

90

BOURBON
WHISKEY

46% ALCOHOL 373

LONDON
FOG

LONDON
FOG

DELICIOUS

Ice Cream

VANILLA

ROSÉ & TONIC

The Rosé & Tonic is a little dry and a little sweet, which makes it a fabulous dinner drink. Pair it with seafood, or any meat or vegetarian dish that features plenty of savoury herbs and spices, and you're in for a real treat. Tonic water has a dry profile and is a natural palate cleanser, so it's always an excellent companion to a meal. Rosé is also a very versatile wine for food pairings, and it contributes a touch of sweetness. The lime brings it all together, adding a hint of tartness both in the drink and on your lips. It's a delightful balance that can make almost any meal more enjoyable.

Ingredients
90ml (3fl oz) rosé
90ml (3fl oz) tonic water
a lime wedge

Instructions
Pour the wine into a tall glass filled with ice, then add the tonic water. Rub the lime wedge around the rim of the glass, then squeeze the juice into the drink and drop the wedge into the glass.

ROSÉ MOJITO

(serves 6–8)

Mojitos are a ton of fun to drink and not as hard to make as you might think. The secret is to use a muddler to press the fresh mint into the syrup. This flavour foundation can then be dressed up in the original way (rum and soda water) or it can take a more unconventional turn, as with the Rosé Mojito. 'Refreshing' doesn't even begin to describe the taste; you'll love how the cooling, sweetened mint plays off a nice rosé. It is then given an extra twist by using a sparkling lemonade rather than soda water. If you prefer it less sweet, add a lemon-flavoured Italian soda water instead.

Ingredients
2 limes, cut into wedges
25g (1oz) fresh mint leaves
Simple Syrup (see page 9), to taste
750ml (25fl oz) rosé
480ml (16fl oz) sparkling lemonade
lime slices and extra mint leaves, to garnish

Instructions
Using a muddler, press the lime wedges, mint leaves and about 15ml (½fl oz) of Simple Syrup in a jug to release the juice and essential oils. Add the rosé and lemonade. Stir well, taste and add more syrup if desired. The jug can then be stored in the fridge for an hour or two. Serve in tall glasses filled with ice and garnish with lime slices and fresh mint.

Tip: If your mint is beginning to wilt, you can make a mint-infused Simple Syrup ahead of time instead. Use a lot of mint so that the flavour is intense – you then won't have to add more syrup later, which would result in an overly sweet drink.

PINK WINE SPRITZER

Sometimes you will open a bottle of rosé only to find that it's not quite what you expected. That doesn't necessarily mean it's bad – it may simply need a little help. In these moments, turn to the Pink Wine Spritzer, a simple recipe that can give any rosé a boost. There are no fancy tricks here, just a little sparkling soda water added to a still rosé. The key is to make sure that both ingredients are well chilled before mixing them. Not only is this a great drink on its own, and fabulously easy to mix up, you will also find it useful if you want to create a cocktail that calls for sparkling rosé, but you don't happen to have a bottle of the bubbly version available. In fact, soda water added to any still wine will allow you to enjoy the same sparkling effect for very little cost.

Ingredients
90ml (3fl oz) chilled rosé
30ml (1fl oz) chilled soda water

Instructions
Pour the rosé into a white-wine glass, then top it off with the ice-cold soda water.

SPICY SPRITZER

Rosé is not out of the question when you're in the mood for a spicy cocktail. You simply have to treat the two flavours in a delicate manner and keep things simple. That's exactly what you'll find in the Spicy Spritzer, a funky twist on the Pink Wine Spritzer (see page 119). The spice in this cocktail comes from a quick infusion of chilli in a citrus vodka. You can use any type of chilli, although Thai chillies and jalapeños are excellent choices. Then, to balance the drink, use soda water if you have a sweeter rosé, or ginger ale if the wine is on the drier side.

Ingredients

2 chillies
45ml (1½fl oz) Citrus-infused Vodka (see page 12)
90ml (3fl oz) rosé
a splash of soda water or ginger ale
an orange slice, to garnish

Instructions

Simply place a couple of chillies in the amount of vodka you'd like to infuse, then taste it after 2 hours. Leave it to infuse a little longer if you'd like it even spicier. This is a fast infusion, so keep testing it and remove the chillies as soon as it reaches your desired intensity. Pour the infused vodka and wine into a tumbler filled with ice. Top with a splash of soda water or ginger ale, stir, and add an orange slice.

ROSÉ COSMO

The classic cosmopolitan is an ideal cocktail for a little rosé. It already has the sweet fruits that pair so nicely with rosé, and the recipe is not too different from the original, so it's both familiar and novel. For the Rosé Cosmo, the wine and citrus vodka play equal roles to form a pretty foundation. This then gets a slight accent from triple sec and cranberry juice to produce a well-balanced cocktail that's easy to drink. In true cosmopolitan fashion, add as much cranberry juice as you like; this recipe produces a drier cosmo that can easily be sweetened by doubling or tripling the juice.

Ingredients
45ml (1½fl oz) Citrus-infused Vodka (see page 12)
45ml (1½fl oz) rosé
15ml (½fl oz) triple sec
15ml (½fl oz) cranberry juice
an orange twist, to garnish

Instructions
Combine the ingredients in a cocktail shaker filled with ice and shake well. Strain into a chilled martini glass and decorate the rim with an orange twist.

LAVENDER PINK LEMONADE

On a hot summer day, nothing is quite as refreshing as a tall glass of lemonade. It's incredibly easy to make lemonade from scratch – all you need is sugar, lemon juice and water. A glass of Lavender Pink Lemonade gives that formula a funky, fresh twist. This recipe begins with a lavender-infused syrup and is best made with freshly squeezed lemon juice. The water of traditional lemonade is then replaced with a good dose of rosé, which turns this popular drink into a stunning wine cocktail for an afternoon in the garden. Though the recipe makes just a single glass, it's easy to mix up for a party. Simply keep the syrup and juice equal at one part each, then use three parts wine. Pour it all into a jug with ice and stir well. Be sure to sample it and adjust the sweet and sour ingredients to suit your taste.

Ingredients
30ml (1fl oz) lavender syrup
30ml (1fl oz) fresh lemon juice
90ml (3fl oz) rosé
a lemon wedge, to garnish

Instructions
Make the lavender syrup in advance by infusing the Simple Syrup recipe on page 9 with 3 tablespoons of lavender flowers. Pour the lavender syrup, lemon juice and rosé into a cocktail shaker filled with ice and shake well. Strain the drink into a highball glass filled with fresh ice and complete it with a lemon wedge.

THE FROSÉ

It may have started as a trend, but The Frosé is a drink that will be enjoyed for many years to come. And if there is one cocktail that rosé is specifically known for, this is it! It has been instrumental in the pink wine's rise in popularity over the last few years. The Frosé is, essentially, a slushie in which you can blend any variety of fruits. The basic recipe features strawberries, which is the best fruit pairing for rosé. You can add the fruit to some Simple Syrup to make a strawberry-flavoured syrup (see page 13 for quantities), but it's much easier to toss it directly into the blender. And a supply of washed, hulled and sliced strawberries (or any fruit of choice) kept in the freezer will make things even quicker. With any frosé, the wine will lose a bit of colour and flavour, so it's best to choose a darker, fuller-flavoured rosé.

Ingredients
332g (11½oz) strawberries, hulled and sliced
150g (5oz) ice
750ml (25fl oz) rosé
2 tbsp white granulated sugar, or to taste
extra strawberry slices, to garnish

Instructions
Put the strawberries and ice in a blender and blitz lightly. Add the rosé and sugar, then blend until smooth. Pour into tall, chilled glasses and garnish with strawberry slices. If it's not thick enough, add a little more ice – you may need as much as 300g (10oz), depending on your preference – and blend again. Likewise, add more sugar if you'd like it sweeter. You can also store any excess frosé in the freezer until you're ready for another drink.

ROSAQUIRI

Freshly made daiquiris beat any mix you can buy from a shop, and the recipe is so simple that it's a shame not to mix one up from scratch. The basic recipe requires rum, lime juice and Simple Syrup, with no secret ingredients. But as you would expect, we're going to add a spin to that recipe to create the fabulous Rosaquiri! Beyond adding rosé wine to the mix, this recipe uses a rosemary-flavoured syrup. It adds a lovely floral note to the cocktail, and you can use any leftover syrup to jazz up a simple glass of lemonade, or to sweeten a wine spritzer (see page 119).

Ingredients

15ml (½fl oz) rosemary syrup
60ml (2fl oz) rosé
45ml (1½fl oz) aged rum
15ml (½fl oz) lime juice
an extra sprig of rosemary and a lime wheel, to garnish

Instructions

Add a sprig or two of rosemary to the Simple Syrup recipe on page 9 and let it steep. Once cool, remove the rosemary from the syrup. Pour the rosemary syrup and all of the other ingredients into a cocktail shaker filled with ice and shake well. Strain into a chilled coupe glass and garnish with a small sprig of rosemary and a lime wheel.

SWEET HONEY ROSÉ

There's a very simple cocktail called the bee's knees that became a hit during Prohibition in America. It was used as a way to doctor up the less-than-desirable 'bathtub' gin of the time by adding honey syrup and lemon juice. The Sweet Honey Rosé reimagines this old-time favourite to create an equally fascinating drink that mixes up in minutes. In this recipe, gin is replaced with whisky – a smooth blend like Irish whiskey is a fantastic choice – and retains the honey syrup and lemon juice. The final ingredient is, of course, rosé. Almost any wine will do and it's best to experiment with a few to find one that matches your taste. Some people may like a sweeter rosé, such as a white zinfandel, while others may prefer a wine with a drier profile.

Ingredients
15ml (½fl oz) honey
15ml (½fl oz) water
45ml (1½fl oz) whisky
a splash of lemon juice
45ml (1½fl oz) rosé

Instructions
There are no secrets to making honey syrup: combine equal parts honey and water and stir until you get a uniform consistency. It's a simple trick that thins out the honey just enough to make it easier to mix in cold drinks. Combine all the ingredients in a cocktail shaker filled with ice. Shake well and strain into a chilled cocktail glass.

SAGE GIMLET

Simple, sophisticated and offering a lovely mix of flavours, the Sage Gimlet puts a wine-and-herb twist on a cocktail that has long been a favourite. Typically, a gimlet is nothing more than gin and lime cordial, and this recipe keeps it fairly simple. The key ingredient here is the sage–lime syrup; adding this to a full-flavoured gin, then finishing it off with a soft rosé creates a cocktail that is perfect for an afternoon in the garden.

Ingredients
15ml (½fl oz) Sage-lime Syrup (see page 12)
45ml (1½fl oz) rosé
45ml (1½fl oz) gin
an extra sage leaf, to garnish

Instructions
Add a few sage leaves and the juice of 1 lime to the Simple Syrup recipe on page 9, then remove the leaves after it cools. In a cocktail shaker filled with ice, combine all the ingredients then shake well. Strain into a chilled cocktail glass and garnish with a single sage leaf floating on top.

SPECIAL

BOURBON

MATURED IN OAK CASKS

43% ALC/VOL

Vol. 700ml

ROSÉ COLLINS

The collins is a classic mixed-drink formula of a base spirit, combined with a sweetener, a sour element and soda water. Any distilled spirit is up for grabs: whisky and gin are the most popular, although vodka, rum and tequila are also good choices. In the Rosé Collins, whisky – specifically bourbon – is the spirit of choice, and the soda water is replaced with a sparkling rosé. The fun elements of this collins are the sweet and sour ingredients. It opts for honey syrup (a mix of equal parts honey and water) along with a muddle of cucumber slices and a lemon wedge. These add a fresh-produce spin on the drink that turns it into an absolute delight for the warmer seasons.

Ingredients
15ml (½fl oz) honey
15ml (½fl oz) water
3 cucumber slices
a lemon wedge
45ml (1½fl oz) bourbon
sparkling rosé, to top up
extra cucumber and lemon slices, to garnish

Instructions
Combine the honey and water and stir until you get a uniform consistency. In a highball glass, muddle the syrup, cucumber slices and lemon wedge. Fill the glass with ice, add the whisky, stir thoroughly, and top up with rosé. Garnish with a slice each of cucumber and lemon.

JASMINE TEA TINI

A tea-flavoured martini is a great choice as an afternoon drink, and jasmine tea is a wonderful, fragrant option. It's particularly nice when paired with rosé in a simple and elegant vodka martini recipe. The Jasmine Tea Tini is easy to prepare and you can adjust each of the elements to suit your personal taste. Start by pouring equal parts of the vodka and rosé, then increase either while reducing the quantity of tea, if you like. Then add more of either the Simple Syrup or lemon juice as you see fit. This is also a lovely recipe to mix up by the jug and serve at a small gathering: keep everything in proportion and increase the pour of each ingredient according to the number of servings you need. You can stir it with ice in the jug, then pour it into cocktail glasses to serve.

Ingredients
30ml (1fl oz) vodka
30ml (1fl oz) rosé
60ml (2fl oz) jasmine tea, chilled
a splash of Simple Syrup (see page 9)
a splash of lemon juice
a jasmine flower or lemon twist, to garnish

Instructions
In a cocktail shaker filled with ice, combine the ingredients. Shake well and strain into a chilled cocktail glass. If available, garnish with a jasmine flower; otherwise use a long lemon twist.

INDEX

YOU CAN'T POUR FROM AN EMPTY CUP.

TAKE CARE OF YOURSELF.

EVERYTHING WILL BE OKAY IN THE END. IF IT'S NOT OKAY, IT'S NOT THE END.

– JOHN LENNON